The Gift

by Lucy Floyd
illustrations by Regan Dunnick

Harcourt Brace & Company

Orlando Atlanta Austin Boston San Francisco Chicago Dallas New York Toronto London

Dad said, "Kent, do you have a gift list?"

"I printed a list," said Kent.

"A pig is last on my list,"
Kent said. "But could my gift
be a pig? Just a little pig?"

So they went to find a pig.
"You are just a runt,"
Kent said.

Runt was the best gift!
Runt ran fast!

Kent kept a soft bed for Runt.
Runt slept there and went
there to rest.

One day Runt left the house.
He ran fast, past a big plant.

"Runt left!" Kent said.
"I must hunt for him!"

"I'll hunt, too," Dad said.
"Let's lift the raft."
But they couldn't find Runt.

Kent bent over the soft bed where Runt slept. He felt so sad.

"Is that a grunt?" Kent asked. "Runt is here! He just ran fast and had to rest!"